JOURNEY #30

Part- 1

Red Jordan Arobateau

Journey #30 —Part 1

Journal #30 in the JOURNEY Series

Any resemblance to any person living or dead is purely coincidental.

All un-attributed quotes are from the Prophet Red Jordan Arobateau.

Published by RED JORDAN PRESS
Redjordanarobateau.com
USA

Am @ Coyote looking @ the presidential debates. Future of our country the rich are dueling it out between them—an absurd 17 candidates.

Nice being w/Jasmin—as she drove me.

See how ignorant the motherfuckers running for office are. All the candidates are rolling down the ramp to their individual podiums—10 of them.

Trump (candidate) speaks out about political correctness—moi agree with that. But international issues, life or death issues are much more important then this thorn in the side.

Some of the candidate contestants really are anti-women rights, would be awful if they won.

Not consider women @ all.

One of them challenges our Hillary Clinton. But he is licking the crotch of communism, — so might not get the nomination for that reason.

These candidates are deceptive and say sanctuary cities should be abolished; however the solution is that our law should be fixed regarding felons. —Not put an end to amnesty for those fleeing for their lives due to persecution by their gender or religion.

These know-nothing Republicans are against sanctuary cities. Against amnesty.

Agitates me when somebody says: *I'll pray for you*—I cringe.

Obama took office promising what America wanted, it was one of his campaign promises to get USA out of foreign war in the Middle East. He kept that promise—which was the people's will. Now these candidates are blaming him for the resultant slaughter there. —

PM
Nada.

Friday, August 7

Am @ Coyote—wrapping up my desk (started last nite) & intend to continue tonight.

Talking politics in the coffee shop. I always seem to find others of my kind.

Talking politics to Josh, —Colorado— & Daria, —Eastern Europe, Moldavia—between customers.

Outside the café windowpane see near traffic collision between 2 pink mustache cabs. These pink moustaches have shrunk—like the mighty dinosaurs devolved into rodents, small mammals—the precursor of our human race—passing up thru the monkey state. (Actually devolved is not a good term, shrinking is more effective because it was highly efficient that the life form continued to live, just made itself smaller.) The moustaches use to be giant, stretching across front grill of car from headlight to headlight.

Sweat was still drying on his back from the walk up.

God showed me wooden cubes—ABC my building blocks as a child.

My spiritual journey is like this today, just higher, far.

Hendrix—Watchtower! Dylan! Twangs, slangs! Responds out of the walls of Coyote.

Brother Leo called. Nice.

Talked to Josh about farming:

> Chickens
> Ducks
> Rabbits
> Vegetables

Misery. Rag pile, peanut butter jar licked clean—by the bus kiosk across from St Francis hospital.

PM
Nada.

Saturday, August 8
There is such an entity as justice. It swings both ways. It swings back into the past and into the future to complete itself. True justice cannot be bought sold nor intimidated—nor under threat—for it to remain justice. In those cases it is transformed into different entity.

> Success is about survival. Its about staying here for the long run.
> --Leonard Cohen musician

PM
Cat's latest fun is to play in my office garbage can. She crawls into it, kicking out much of the contents. Then lays atop or half in, flattening it out. So this means hours later when she has abandon it, I have to bend down and PU all the trash and unflatten the bag and stick all the crap back inside—very unnecessary time consuming!

Sunday, August 9
Sermon by our new dean:

> Walt Whitman always carried a pencil, in his back pocket, or his
> hat; he walked the area around 10 miles around his house taking
> notes for his journal: I am a watchman watching for God.

Annie & I went to Mel's restaurant & whooped w/fun. @ one point the conversation as always took a serious twist, & we talked about the heinous Isis, which is ironically, the name of a female deity—but is the Islamic hater-murderous thugs sweeping across the middle east, Syria in particular; and Annie said it was going along @ a lower & lower level. Caging captives then setting fire to them, drowning captives in cages.

They are sinking lower & lower, so that it is now apparent they are serving the devil and not Islam in one bit—unless Islam *is* the devil, which is an idea awful to consider.

Annie & I also spoke of the great conflict she feels in Grace—a Christen church, so very accepting, after being brainwashed and

5

raised in a Hong Kong evangelistic Christian haters church, which assured them several times per day they were going to hell…

I told her it was the evangelisticals who had taught those Christian schools, just as it is the evangelists infiltrating and seizing religious power in Uganda, training the black people there to loathe gays, and conditions for gays in Uganda has gone from bad to worse. Then I told her about the thought I'd had earlier this week:

> Agitates me when a Christian says: *I'll pray for you* — cringe. *I'll pray for you*. And it terrifies me.

PM
Nada.

Monday, August 10
Am @ Coyote. Must loose weight. Stop eating. Lord/ess told me 3 weeks ago.

Am outside Coyote. ½ banana, ½ sweetened coffee, a sparkling water, 1 hardboiled egg—

Must get closer to the Garden.

Talked to lady cabdriver, Margo. Laughs—about foibles of this city—chiefly its $ grabbing.

Sky dark, dreary twilight approaches.

Très fatigue says young foreign child passing by w/her parents.

PM
Nada.

Tuesday, August 11
Went to Coyote. Fortunate enough to find another person to speak to for several hours—OGM Tom.

PM
I have the thought for the first time in my life, in this manner: you are wrapping up things on earth, getting ready for the next life. And it

6

seems to be approaching a happy vacation, an adventure, a place of joy to come, w/no fear—a transition not an end, of course.

Wednesday, August 12
Shrink.

Coyote has gone so downhill. Talked to many.
They all agree.

A white ape-man half naked runs down center of Polk Street, bent over double, begging money to drivers in their windows of cars that pass.

On wei bible study.

> I am as fierce; Like a bear robbed of her cubs!
> --God in Hosea

One here who de sexes all the few She's into He's.

Unplesant, and pushing me to start saying aloud She for everything. Which is war.

I Am who I Am. —Exodus 3 13-15.

Eminent & transcendent fish in water.

Before he opened the tan wood door to the sanctuary: *would you come to see Me?* God said. He opened the door to the Most High.

By now OM had driven so many people from himself, he had messed up others reading of him as to his true ideas and compassions.

PM
Nada.

Thursday, August 13
Here I sit inside Coyote; sat in. Coffee, ice water. Daydreaming movie scores.

Me am now outside; sat in de sun arms bare sun-collecting.

7

Go outside, immediately mentally ill person goes to the table next to mine, mumbling to himself. Its very difficult to be surrounded by this.

Another lightskin brother, tan skin, curly, not kinky hair.

Another driven crazy light skin bro spat out of the ghetto.

Bro sits there using the owners ketchup on some hot dogs someone else has left out on the table—in the sun 2 hours— not a good idea, plenty of time for bacteria to grow.

They have nothing but the space they inhabit.

And use this to irritate anybody sane.

PM
Anne H. calls, tells me she has a job interview tomorrow AM—it is a menial job, for the City—to me this is a very good job, but not to her, and for her perceived opinion of herselfs station in life and what those relatives (Chine—aghast) and acquaintance @ church *might think.* Good luck to her—it is a good plan!

Is applying for a job—I can't say what kind! She has forbidden me— but me trés glad about this break thru!

Friday, August 14
Sam calls—soon to arrive. Just got to Coyote—no homeless out here crazy-acting. Many young healthy out here—

PM
In the Ho's obtaining cooked fish for my din(s) next two days—Annie Ho calls: *I can't take the job, sorry. It is too awful. Cleaning up shit—dog shit—even human shit. You know how I am, you know I cannot do that.* I should have realized this.

Street cleaning job.

Job benefits are not bad! People in this city begging for a job!

Dr. Sam told me a hideous story:

8

> A young female student went to the Middle East to be an aid for Doctors Without Borders in one of those impoverished nations. She was kidnapped by Isis to be a wife for one of the Isis generals. She was raped every night by 5 or 6 men—friends of his, and died after 2 years.

More horror added to the present knowledge we already have.

In yesterdays news a young black American woman, just graduated w/top honors from high school, and her Middle Eastern boyfriend—son of an Imam—who just graduated from college were caught @ the Florida airport—on their way to join Isis for their honeymoon.

They are being held w/no bail.

I repeat they were on their way: *to join Isis for their honeymoon.*

Whaaaaat? Can these kids be thinking?

Saturday, August 15
Stayed home again today—3rd Sat in a row. Rest!

Watch nature program on Public Broadcasting System—Crows!

PM
Nada.

Sunday, August 16
The OM sat on a fire hydrant praying on the wei to church:

Where is my job?

The TM was hungry for it.

Coming.

BONG! BONG! BONG! The bells chime.

PM

Oh, did I tell you Megan has shed new boyfriend—they have nothing in common.

Monday, August 17
Spoke w/old man writer outside Café, in childhood he had 2 near death experiences. —*I was much more positive after that. I think that's what has made me positive, optimistic all my life.*

Sitting here thinking about my sexual orientation—mostly women—females.

Kindness.

Mentioned to this old man I belonged to a GLBT church, soon he gets up & walks away.

God is not just better, God is higher.

If you are higher you will be better.

PM
Arabic women who have voluntary joined Isis have a higher status then those kidnapped; they have higher duties—they marry the fighters, they stand guard @ checkpoints, they manage the rape brothels.

After hearing this term on PBS news, Google searched it—to find it is true, the highest premium female jihad fighters of Isis are British born Islamic, they are used to manage/guard the rape brothels—the chief victims in them currently are the Yhseazdic women who, tho Arab and Islamic, are considered by the jihadists to be non Islamic, and non human and the Isis interpretation of the Koran allows them to do anything they want to inferior females.

This is sick.

Just emerging is this information of the place of value some females have—now it is more apparent why a female, any female, would join Isis—knowing she is not going to be raped 30 times a day until she is dead—like captive females.

Unspeakable horror.

The world must unite to destroy this Isis, just as they did to Hitler and his concentration camps. The world waited so long, America dragging its feet—in that time millions of Jews and others were tortured and murdered, burnt in ovens, went up in smoke.

Part of their death rate is suicide. The captive females of Isis are killing themselves to escape the rape torture.

Again I say, America has so much power, but is so slow to act—in concert with half a dozen other nations who are ready and fighting Isis already!

Tuesday, August 18
Am @ Coyote. First fight of the day @ small market.

Am @ the café. Spoke w/nice woman been a schoolteacher 4 years in Indonesia:

> — Indonesia is poor—but the people are nice. America has a way of trying to fix its problems, all over—w/temporary solutions, bandaids, not solutions that will work.
>
> The insane homeless you see here—don't see in Indonesia, the family structure is strong, they take their poor in.

They po', wei po' some all they want is that empty cup they think you ready to throw out-but yo's po', yo' need it too!

Oh the pain in my legs.

Found miss-mash different food in a sack abandon @ bus kiosk— took it must cook well!

PM
Well to be quite honest this homeless situation is insane. New laws to prevent homeless *from sleeping on the street!* Whenever you have medical or scientific research projects shown on TV about sleep deprivation you see what a major problem it is for those who can't sleep! Yet the City would stop people from sleeping in the streets—

and they cannot afford housing! What are they suppose to do? The homeless shelters fill up and —hundreds are turned away! All humanbeings have to sleep! It can drive a human crazy not having enough sleep! These people have no money, nowhere to go, no home to return to, no family who will accept them. Many are orphans who never had any family!

Big titties! Eee ohhh!

Wednesday, August 19
2nd story going in thick mental sheets, huge boisterous girders pile drive into bedrock—the new hospital.

Shrink.

Me & therapist L., spoke of N'Orleans:

> Crocodiles
> Humid heat like a wet blanket in front of your face
> Oil wells on property next door to your house
> Murder rate

The bus kiosk stank of piss. He rested on a plastic seat. Resting his ass. Heavy-laden pack and aluminum cane.

Am @ Coyote. Me so tired.

Spoke to barista E, of Romania, Ukraine Kazakhstan et al—

> I think they are fighting there…

> Who Isis? Or Russia?

> Russia.

> Which is worse Russia or Isis?

She pondered over this.

> Its between 2 devils.

What Isis is doing is mastery of the most barbaric principals.

Neighborhood meeting man came in paid me a compliment—said I looked very nice—am wearing matching trousers & shirt!

Well the wheels are turning in this city, in this nation, this neighborhood—upcoming elections.

SF Mayor is under police investigation, and the big one the sweeping one—national election for prez.

Am waiting for neighborhood meeting w/the current sheriff—w/food? Then bible study.

Me am so tired.

The tranny girls have obtained a baby stroller & now 3 furry heads of their dogs all piled into it, are visible as they look about, passing by.

Yum, Yemeni oeuveres.

We studied:

> Mark 14, 12
> Mathew 8; 5-13
> Luke 7; 1-10.

Anything's liable to happen & @ any time:

> God will appear
> Earthquake strike

PM
Nada.

God/ess does not give us the things we want (Lotto).

I give you –*The things I ordain you to have.*

Thursday, August 20

Got to Coyote—found homeless had snatched tips from the tip jar and run off w/it.

These maladjusted sociopaths cannot keep preying on these people— these providers for the area, especially not underpaid non insured baristas!

A man. He was white, bald.

Good hot bible study last nite!

Sun was warm—briefly—on the walk up.

Did I say am @ Coyote—no sun; marine layer full 2,000 miles thick, not hot—thank God.

Dear Lord/ess You're right & I know nothing,

Saw DVM he doing very well—instillation commission, wheat pastes, then painting off of this, and pop outs, down in Del Mar $3,000!

Said our book might not come out in September: *I thought it was in October.*

Oh the other day man told me about his engineering project: *if I don't do it in 7 years—I'll never do it. I'll no longer have the desire. I just won't care anymore*

A simply amazing & unexpected thing happened today.

As walked out of café and down the block along the building front— passing Hawk and her sweet large poodle:

> Hey—I forgive you.
>
> Oh, well I forgive you too…
>
> Oh! You said it so quick…

That's because of I forever bow @ the communion fountain &
cleanse my soul.

PM
Nada.

Friday, August 21
Saw Peter Grace, told him about the scriptures— that you have this
particular man carrying a jug of water & men didn't use to carry
water. –Only women, or male or female slaves. This means the man
was purposefully taking on a woman's role. He was transgender!

He had never heard of it quite like that before!

Am @ Coyote now: it is a cool wind like fall blowing in the door—
jacket off—but am sweaty from my 7.5 block walk. So it is a draft.

Watched out window as 2 homeless turned down the alley, one was
pissing between 2 parked cars, but police were on them, turned down
the alley too, and as they were being confronted, who walks in the
café door and sits beside me—Joe—(Rent boy); looks good—very
good. Hair streaked blond. Body perfect from weightlifting. Wore
dark trousers & hoodie w/HUSTLER! Written on the front. Sat
perched on barstool and I gave him a fiver to buy himself a coffee, he
kept the change. Thought about his hot thighs, his warm bod his neat
package of nuts and dick in his crotch. Oh, Joe made a funny:

> You sleeping in the alley?

> I look @ it more like camping out these days.

He is doing well—*partially off heroin*—and sometimes working as a
roofer. He lives with a girlfriend and they have their own apartment.
(Down the peninsula.) This is very much better. He says he will be
in town awhile.

PM
Nada.

Saturday, August 22
Slept in, late 6PM, now up to sto' for food.

Oh, I had a dream. I was in one of the old Victorian flats—w/many rooms, & circular living room windows overlooking street, expensive; it was full of pleasant people, some religious peeps. I went into a room in front w/people; I was talking to a man, very advanced, maybe Transman, who held a high church position, immediately I saw laying over a sturdy antique armchair, an extremely expensive suit—trousers, jacket, satiny, white— a glistening white. The tranny religious man indicated I should try it on—I had on some rather nice trousers already, but did not have a jacket, I slipped on the elegant white silver trousers on over my others, and the waist just buckled, not too large. The jacket was for me also. I awoke.

Would I put on these clothes? These were the clothes the Eternal has prepared for Her-His servant, they are of a much better, finer quality then anything I have in my current wardrobe—or ever have possessed. I was going to be advanced into a higher position, and needed these clothes to fulfill my job in it.

PM
I hurt, I really hurt because of the small hairy rhino declared extinct in Malaysia.

Malaysia is certainly a stupid country.

Sunday, August 23
Am making my wei uphill to Grace; heard from congregant I see frequently in the street (art show) about another congregant who has taken vows:

> There he was all dressed in white w/shaved head—he took his vows order of Episcopal monastics, Christ, obedience, poverty. The Episcopal's order is small — 140 of them all over the USA— his lodgings is up in XX; just him lives there. Their order gets together 2 times a year!

My order DOC would be living together.

Jim @ church:

16

I live in Montclair; in the yards of Montclair there are a lot of rats. People started using rat poison—and it killed the rats—their corpses were eaten by other wildlife—including owls. All of a sudden there was no more owl population—owls are a natural predator of rats. And yes, the rat population exploded! So they went back to the old trap-and-kill method. Sure enough the owl population has returned to Montclair.

Had been thinking about robins—then amid the gothic grey brick backdrop, he saw a red robin hop among the ferns/greenery, vegetation in hunt for a twilight meal. OM prayed: *God/ess let her-him find a worm.*

The downwinds to streets are a clean & empty of all riff raff; removed those bad homeless, then in this emptiness is invisible jaws—that lay in wait to devour me too—us; all of us outcasted by social norms.

PM
Took testosterone shot. Lifted my weights, moved my Journal forward by several pages of the day, lived.

Monday, August 24
Am @ Coyote, gave biz card to Daria, told her I am GLBT, spoke w/the young lady she has driven social media in the past.

You have a biz; Hashem told the OM—*don't forget about it—*

The Puerto Rican tranny saunters out of de alley holding the top of her red skirt over the lower part of her face—the more masculine part—as a disguise, then she goes back past—she is walking on the tips of he toes like she would if she had on high heels—what a spectacle—what a heartache.

How deep is your love?

Sit here in the last waning hours of Coyote, spoke to Hawk, and her giant Poodle of note—spoke w/pleasant barista Daria both on the biz card warned her about queer stuff if she should look @ if she is interested—the art paintings website, and she could drive my site.

17

Lucky you wern't here yesterday it was crazy; homeless outside homeless they come inside they steal, I cant watch everything.

See the now bare café stripped of its I-pad, and its computers, by common thieves who broke in @ nite.

PM
Came across this from WORD NO, originally from my collection of 800-poems:

In our assemblies
Where the word is NO.
The noise we make is…
NOTHING.
See! You all,
Glaring, with the soil on your hands!
Unrelated
To the odd
Incidents
of power.
(not by Voodoo, or sorcery.
Magic with no wands.)

People wake up!
We're super human!
Skulls dripping blood from human thorns.

Our language is full of holes
That gums deride.
But, in unguarded moments—in fogs;
Impetuous
Secret, inside your heart,
Latent,
Far from your sucking eye
That leapfrogs
Stuck within the Apparentness of cement,
Read between the lines—
Of unreality. Thin structures
From which you're longing to explode!

--In the Acid Palace

Tuesday, August 25

Am @ Coyote outdoors, Jasmin cut hair/beard; thinking about Jesus in the upper room.

Your hermitage has been a lonely thing because you're not in community.

You are utterly alone—w/God...

After a reading the homo scriptures this morning—Jesus seeking out the queer man (on his way w/a jug of water) obvious familiarity w/him & his home where he lived w/his master, where the Passover would be kept, Jesus' obvious acceptance of this.

One of the gals here—from Kazakhstan—pray for her she gets a job in her field, as she has recently graduated—in social welfare for women/girls, globally.

Am @ Coyote—spoke to several Rooski gals behind counter. Eastern European.

Outdoors, one so young—full head of hair, blanket draped over his shoulders barechest & super too large trousers.

His face is a worried frown—even tho he is so handsome. A worried brow; ever-twisting lips in unheard conversation w/his devils.

The conditions of hu(man) rise up—they come & go out of this; God extends the souls. Have faith in God in all things—problems @/making friends in companionship—among:

> Strangers
> Regulars
> Workers behind the counter

—as they come & go as if thru a revolving door.

Talked to Daria—maybe leaving here.

19

PM
Nada.

Wednesday, August 26
Shrink.

Am @ Coyote.

Young man raised by single mom he may grow up hating women—resenting his mom—her power over him, his own dependence on her, he refuses to see her pain.

The 3 Latina transgenders and 1 gay boy walk down Polk—Mami walks her 3 poodles miniatures—in a baby carriage—their furry heads can be seen looking about like movie stars in their convertible car.

Day dreaming movie scenario this one wei funny slapstick.

Well tomorrow maybe D-day when a certain person I showed biz card to (trans outing) returns to work & see her reaction—subtle rejection is 90% the case of the time.

Waiting for 5PM to go to church.

So what happens to those so mentally disabled & now out in the street?

How deep is your love?
How deep is your love?

Always look for the forgotten ones.

Qyuan Yen would say something like that.

I first heard about Quan Yen in my shrink's office—a little shrine to her w/water in a pleasant flowing fountain over beautiful smooth round stones. There she was, a serene Asian Madonna draped in flowing robes, standing in the grotto.

20

Then heard more from Chinee friend Annie Ho, we were in a Chinese restaurant and they had statue of the warrior god—you've seen it. A huge cruel face w/snarl & large mustache; carrying a scimitar sword.

This is common in businesses. You see him—this to protect their business. Then they'll have another one, usually Quan Yen as well.

Hers is bigger and higher, reclusive back up in the wall.

PM
Nada.

Thursday, August 27

> He's a shooter I like a shooter—all over my face, my chest...
> --XX, (OGM)

PM
Nada.

Friday, August 28.

PM
Nada.

Saturday, August 29
Stayed in, day of rest all day—as planned. Got some small tasks accomplished. Green & White out again.

PM
Nada.

Sunday, August 30
Church. Walked to the pulpit to read my scripture. Alors! It was James, and not Deuteronomy as had been planned, and practiced! Well people said I'd carried off a cold reading very well.

Thanks be to God/ess!

PM
Art site payment will be due on September 9th. I'm prepared for it this year!

Monday, August 31

Am @ Coyote. Saw David Steinberg (photographer, artistic photographer, fetish, gender photographer, writer) @ WallGrims, he is in our book! –Allen Kaufman's Outlaw Bible of Artists—artists and apparently photogs as well.

Sun blazes bright.

He sits in Diva's often during the week. As I sit here in Miss Coyote.

PM
Delicious episode of Frinye Fisher—Miss Fisher's Murder Mysteries—out of Australia & the UK. Lesbian doctor Mack dressed in masculine suits, is friend of Lady Dick, Miss Fisher—staring Essie Davis, so hot! Mack's lesbian relationship w/young female factory worker woman is revealed—Lesbianism is a crime in its time, 1930's. The hot hug and caresses between Essie & Mack is very emotional near the end of this episode. Yum.

We need so much more of this transgressive lesbian visual representation, isn't the public kinda bored of the same old straight shit?

Oh, on news more ancient Roman buildings destroyed in Syria—2,000 years antiquity—this is cutting down Syria's future! In archeology, in tourism, in education.

Oh. Saw Joe @ Coffee shop—he a wreck—in drug yen or some chemical state of physical disintegration. Told him point blank: *I have no money. This is rent-paying week.*

Two people are looking for Joe for a date, —want me to get his phonenumber, but he has no phone!

Tuesday, September 1
Am @ Dr.s office. Tall black man, (lite colored), loud & threatening. Rude, try's to push ahead of me @ check in desk, makes my blood boil. He begins yelling @ the check in clerk. Burly white-Mex guard in uniform strides over, walks him outside out of the waiting room into the plaza into the open air.

WELL WHAT I DID? WHAT I DID?

The man walks back inside the waiting room, followed by the guard.

Pick up your script!

Pick up your script!

WHAT'S THE PROBLEM! I GOTTA COME HERE & COMMIT A CRIME!

Sit down!

AH AIN'T GONNA SIT DOWN!

Well stand then. Says the guard walking away, trying to cool the situation.

I COULD SEE IF I DONE SOMETHING WRONG! DON'T MAKE NO FUCKEN' SENSE!

@ this point the guard approaches the nearly-out-of-control asshole once again, pointing @ the man to sit down—and the brother chooses to walk towards TM to sit by him.

I'M NOT SITTEN' HERE! Yells Transman, getting away from him. I'M NOT SITTING HERE, I'M NOT SITTIN' HERE!

I NEVER GET HARASSED LIKE THIS! THIS SOME BULL SHIT! I KNOW MY FUCKEN' RIGHTS! —I GONNA SAY WHAT I WANT TO SAY!

PM
Nada.

Wednesday, September 2
Thank you God, I am here. —Coyote.

Walked up from shrink—24 blocks.

23

A madman, meth-head (sadly) shuffles along the street, the gaze in his head permanently affixed to the cement sidewalk before him—he carries in his arms some junk-treasures already found. His footfalls stop, he bends over—PU the branch of a flower stalk w/dried leaves—relishes it holistic—sees it deeply. He stares at it, fully for minutes, unmoving on the street.

They look @ us as a sexy woman or hot man; is that all we are, sum & total, genitalia that can hold in the palm of your hand?

I remember…

Here I am church bible study, gay laughter from inner office.

I'm always overlooked.

Thousands of years passed in oral histories. The Hebrew tribe began writing down Torah around 700 BC.

I have been loud enough; said the OM.

@ one point a OM really began to see God/ess grants gifts some not readily apparent—that people saw him as not popular—so he could <u>see!</u>

PM
Human flesh is corrupt. Human thoughts are corrupt.

>They're calling on their mothers, they're calling on God. Its mass confusion.
>--The Civil War

**

>Everything in the planet is
> gone.
>Just a skull.
> A dry empty wind
> blowing.

>We are your false pupils.

The deadliest
Warriors.

Thursday, September 3,
@ Coyote after whirlwind ride w/Jasmin drive to pay RENT.

Roooski male talks in a loud deep voice: *da! DA! DA!*

Sun blazes; event @ Grace soon.

However wind blows cool.

Jasmin drives back/forth Polk to pay RENT no funds & she gave me $200, as I was short.

Ah! Life in the big city!

I remember the blazing hot summer days of NYC the Village –when the Village had Nathan's pushcart hotdog venders, $1. Hotdogs heaping w/sauerkraut & mustard.

This is such a stable country & I am so grateful for it—I look @ the city buildings—her ledges upon which to sit; grey sidewalks that go everywhere & all places for all people to walk. I thank God/ess for my freedom—my American freedom.

Nearly time to depart for Grace to partake in nightly nosh, Evensong service, & welcoming the new dean.

By 2015 the cathedral had a new dean…

Hey goood looking! Comes a voice to Transman's reverie—in an ocean of sun. It is the woman from a rich family, paid $ to stay away, to live an independent life out here in poverty, in an SRO.

In friendly SF.

Wind blows stronger.

TM got a good sun. Oh, good jerk off last nite!

And these are my religious works?

Pretty blax gal slides by in diaphanous sienna garment & combat boots. She smells so good! Her perfume lingers in the air. Buttery brown skin. Dreads coiled right down her neck like snakes.

One by one, two by two, affluent young people in colorful sports clothes march past—they are all such good spirits. However every 10th person is homeless & a bum scuffling on broken feet, grisly faced, draped in a blanket of overt shame.

Oh, sat out here w/2 man-lovers, watching vidios of their man trade w/dicks in foreign lands (sex tourism—the 18 year old to 23 variety).

You haven't far to go, do you recall how I came to you out of the clouds of eternity?

Evensong.

The choir sings *God/ess be praised!* Its resonant masculine voices—

Well let me tell you about that day—Wednesday, sat w/all men @ picnic tables, speaking of male sex, dicks, trade; and then in bible study reading aloud all man scriptures not any validation of me as a trans man, or any feminism ethic.

Well don't stop asking for what you want/need.

The Lord/ess loves justice the Lord/ess loves Her special ones.

The love of God in their hearts.

Why aren't more people here? The OM entertained this thought many times, gazing about the holy places he went. Rows of empty chairs prepared for a congregation, which only sparsely appears. For in that time, and in that town, in the 21st century, there had been a great, great falling away of the people from the One who had created them.

My soul does magnify the Lord/ess.

OM spent much of the service puzzling at conversation like a sit com between readings from the bible & musing out his faith from the choir.

It was hot.

PM
Nada.

Friday, September 4
We are born into trouble.

Am @ Coyote in the sun. Straight man talked to in the past, then mentioned queer issues, says hello—then runs away.

Sit w/no $; thankfully RENT paid but now computer has issues.

> Do I look like a straight man?
> —Zero Mostel

So Meg Wolf just gave me instructions how to reset my computer w/icons in place.

On way to church. Meeting about GLBT persecution in Africa, w/Nigerian gay man.

Some horrifying sports game is going on in tavern across street—

> OUHHHH!

> AHHHHHH!

A keen-eyed bird sits on top ledge; I am underneath—this far down, there is no barbed wire — bird preens feathers black grey violet, green majestic.

Am seated down @ far end.

Will learn what I can pour moi for my journal (from Journal of days of Red J Arobateau) and go home & reboot—I have a work to do for Christ.

Stopped outward are cues to the inward soul—coming up thru layers of conscious to you to discover from within.

Am @ presentation—but no one is here.

A big sissy arrived w/a fan.

Really have earned what I have. All the challenges I accept.

—No one is here—yet must endure it for the info, the enlightenment.

Nigeria is very homophobic—it is dangerous to be gay there. Uganda is easier, South Africa, Senegal. Nigeria is oil rich—it can do what it wants to do. So it can afford to hate, to murder, w/out risking their status. Many other African nations depend on foreign aid, tourism, for money so they cannot be too homophobic—least their funds be cut off.

The early Africans weren't homophobic. Their recognized gay as just a part of human life—which occurred in every generation—it was not until the advent of Christianity—the white man's influence that this queer hate began.

It is ironic. Always chastise us saying; *don't preach that gay stuff, that is the white mans disease.* But as we know there are plenty of home grown African gays—and it is the white mans Christianity which first labeled it a sin.

He got out of the meeting @ 9PM.

The man who walks up & down is still walking up & down.

PM
Nada.

Saturday, September 5

Stayed home all day—slept, rested, Green & White out. Some very basic work on Journals.

PM
His sex toys were still steaming hot from his body. The OM, heaved a sigh of relief. His night awaited him—w/parrots on each shoulder; Green on his place, White on hers.

5AM watched a bit of the Grapes of Wrath (John Steinbeck, novelist, socialist) in it a destitute man, on the dusty road is the former preacher of the area—he says: *I've lost the Spirit—what good am I now? I can't be a preacher no more, since I lost the Holy Spirit.*

Sunday, September 6, Fifteenth Sunday After Pentecost
Everyone is nice & says hello to me.

Cold gothic stone. Coat on.

PM
Nada.

Monday, September 6,
The seasons change. Blazing hot now—soon will be winter.

Am out here in the heat—wow. Spoke to Hawk & petted her sweet gigantic poodle dog.

Finally a wind blows!

Steady, strong!

Middleage man tips by in taut satin tights, his junk, rounded, bobs, paramount in his crotch.

PM
Nada.

Tuesday, September 8
Out in heat, got exercise. Sat @ Coyote, talked to railroad (straight) man in parklet, then walked home. Nearly 95 degrees—but mercifully a wind blew.

Oh, did I mention, the Palestinian nephew who manages the café is back. Is this good news or bad?

PM
Nada.

Wednesday, September 9
Shrink. The OM spoke of Rentboy.com being busted & taken down off the Internet—and bible study coming up that evening, over which he was expectant—both in the same breath:

> You have such a well-rounded life.
> --L., Therapist

PM
Nada.

Thursday, September 10
Beautiful sounds choir still singing on high from hallway behind us; so encompassing the high church robed choir faded in distance, yet by their angelic sound remained.

Ladies smoozing & blocking the aisle.

Heard some astounding news; seated in the dining room w/XX, we w/balanced plates of hor d'oeuveres on our laps, noshing:

> The history of our church is shady—many estate trusts are built on money earned during the slave trading years.
>
> As slave owners.
>
> No; as slave traders. The people who went to Africa purchased slaves and brought them back to America, quite a few huge fortunes were massed from this, and are funding the financial wheels of the Episcopal church today.

PM
Nada.

Friday, September 11

Walked to Café, talked to some, have not spent a sou inside all week, I think my new little friend Josh may be departed.

This hot weather has been murder, it is getting windier, and cooler, thank God/ess.

PM
You see I have another problem w/my life—my career! One area unresolved—Having worked so long and put in so many hours to have gained next to no public acclaim!

Sometime I feel I'm carrying the pain of the world around inside my body. Twist and shake my head—@ the sight of murder of elephants in South Africa—by shooting them from helicopters.

Put up WORD NO hardcopy on Text POD.

Shake, shake, shake—those titties!

Saturday, September 12
Day off—stayed home. No trek to coffee shop. Puttering around house.

PM
Nada.

Sunday, September 13, The Sixteenth Sunday After Pentecost
The wind is cold, whipping up Taylor Street—on wei to Grace.

I know OM thought of the other day, younger OGM who told the tale of one younger OGM and himself:

> I went to Brazil and got drunk, I had on my cargo pants w/100 bills in the front left pocket, $50 in the front right, and $20's and $10's & fives in the back. I left all the singles on the bar for tips. When I was dancing I was pulling out the money to pay for drinks for me & my boy and my friends, and all the money got mixed up and some of it got danced out and fell onto the floor when I woke up the next morning I didn't have nothing left...

I was young, 16, and in a New York Mafia Gay bar. I had $100, which was a lot for me. I bought drinks and was stuffing my change back into various pockets, front, back, and lost track of it, and some of it fell out onto the floor I was dancing so hard. When I woke up the next morning all I had was carfare home.

Flock of pigeons are having a fest atop Diocesan House chimney— maybe it is still warm.

The parishioner who sighs randomly w/boredom, deep, disruptive groans & sighs strolls about the plaza talking to herself including a few poignant *Fuck You's* she wears a diaphanous top.

Fog settles on the cathedral, her spires, her latticework frieze parapets, her bell tower, her crucifix spire, her radically slanted roofs. Pale grey sky closes in obscura.

Fog moving in enveloping—grey, —bringing droplets of rain. OM realized he'd worn his sun screen to no avail.

Strong—sun breaks, blazing, golden & brazen thru grey overcast just over the west wing of the West transept & the edge of 2nd floor boys school offices, sinking into that crevice there then moving off in hint of rouge then gone.

Toot far reaching; foghorn warning tug boats in the bay.

Fog hangs obscure covering all the big fancy hotels up here on the top of the hill.

Pigeons squat, preen & chortle on the chimney.

W/my good eye closed can still see enough to walk.

My body is breaking down. I am old.

Entered the cool lofty space. He saw the bible, its red cover open on the communion table. *I've been speaking to you thru the centuries.*

The bells chime.

32

Walked down hill towards grocery sto' then home.

Cold wind in my face. Cold such a welcome relief after the murderous heat.

PM

> Write about what you know, what you are familiar w/& then add to it w/your imagination. That's what I've done.
> --Red Jordan Arobateau, Author, Painter, Spiritual Seeker

Monday, September 14
Approach Coyote see youth who looked so well last week, his hair trimmed, beard trimmed, clothes neat—now gone wild; trouser legs stepped on ripped to rags, flapping, both feet bare, hair/beard wild, shaking his head—he is off his meds, and high on crank.

A lonely miserable day out here; evil wheelchair man inside—no friends & no friendly baristas. The owner's nephew is serving.

Bums squat outside, bum woman sits @ table next to mine, exams left-over plates for food—bums cigarette, bums a light—blows smoke, which blows in my face.

PM
Watched Agnes of God, TV, w/Jane Fonda; all nuns in black/white habits running around the screen—holy cinematography.

Tuesday, September 15
Seated outside Coyote—after dentist.

In a table out here by myself.

Cold today—so much better then last week sun unbearable heat.

I have gone from one poverty scene—Capp off 16th, Native American dentist, w/derelict bodies, beggars, dope dealers hidden in recesses of buildings blankets over their shoulders native style, to Miss Polk Strassa—in Tendernob district, along destitute row, but also many upscale walk past.

Fog settling in.

Well Fall is approaching—my time—cold rain in the air, the drab streets where many personalities circulate.

PM
Weightlift.

Wednesday, September 15
Here I be—out here @ Coyote.

> And behold there came up out of the river seven fat beautiful cows,
> and they fed in a meadow.
> And, behold seven other cows came up after them, poor and very
> ugly and skinny, such as I never saw in all the land of Egypt or
> badness.
> And the skinny ugly cows ate up the first seven fat beautiful cows.
> —Genesis 41 14 17-21

PM
Nada.

Thursday, September 17
Went out late to Coyote—check arrived—money is mine! Spoke w/Kurt.

PM
Sent off Text POD order for Bancroft.

Got email fan letter from Transman in publishing industry.

Friday, September 18
The Lord/ess told me something encouraging:

When you *go home & work on My book* tonite.

So I'm doing something! W/all this scribbling!

Ahhh Ahhmen! Ahhhhhmen!

Mad traffic cascades down Bush Street racing honking @ each other.

Young white male naked from waist up full head of wild hair, digs into garbage can, produces a bottle—tips it up, drinks. *Fool;* thought TM laughing sympathizing @ the irony of this totally lost soul amid all the sophisticated tekkies; thought of his state, and thru it racing, honking, jousting for first position, meaningless posturing are worse fools.

Am in Coyote glad walked up on sunny side of the street—due to the fact there is no sun left out here—having coffee & soon return home to do God/esses Will, as instructed above.

There is a creature seated outside spewing race hate out of his foul mouth in a deep gravelly voice—; caught this in a draft, race thoughts of his thuggish mind: *uh, uh, nigas favoring white boys; talks to a white boy befo' a nigga.*

And this fool is talking about me!

The soul returns to God—others have worked hard and are harmless—& gain.

Spoke w/Crash, he showed me a new exercise to do amid my weights—a partial pushup.

Crash—handsome young personal trainer, motorcycle instructor.

PM
Nada.

Saturday, September 19
One thing I have learned from last Wednesdays Bible Study—God will fulfill all Her/His promises to us. Sara was barren, her menstrual cycle had ceased, her estrogen had plummeted; she was 80 years old—yet God/ess gave her a child. The thing she had hoped for so long was granted to her!

Daughter!

PM

This world drags on; but that worlds so beautiful a place, such a joyous realm, w/dancing, singing, self-expression to the fullest.

Sunday, September 20
After the food, the laughter, only the serious remain for evening service.

Those who care in even deeper even more profound regions have made their way here.

PM
Nada.

Monday, September 21
Am @ Coyote. Immediately a mad man sits down—talking to himself—so unpleasant.

> I walk the streets people view me, say its my fault! I ain't did nothing. I walk these streets—I don't bother nobody!

Artist (musician) colleague of mine has got a parttime job. He works as a floor walker @ strip club.

*$40, she can be your*s. He says, sarcastically.

Sit here awaiting cooler weather.

Fall—a time to work.

Humans do a lot of very bad things, yet also so many good—like they strung colored lights between Lower Fern Alley & Upper—hung between two light posts across Polk Strassa. How beautiful they are when dusk falls: green, gold, red, blue. Dreams of Christmas joy, of magical presents.

Betty Smith another novelist/playwright, must this say again A Tree Grows In Brooklyn is a magnificent book—it has got all the elements. A poor wife's soul hardening because of the trials of life—a singing waiter lost in fantasy who builds castles in the sky to escape life, while becoming a hopeless drunk, a girl who can use fantasy to create wonderful art.

PM

The race-card delivered its little stinging slap yesterday. The woman I was speaking w/viewed one of our new priests, a handsome chocolate skin Blackman w/luxurious braids down his back (probably gay). On commenting to this new addition to the clergy:

> You know I'm part black.
>
> No!
>
> Yes!
>
> No you <u>aren't</u>!
>
> My mother was light skin black!

Silence.

So this from someone I've known 9 years—on a casual basis.

God this aggravates me!

Back in the small towns of the south where we were from, everybody would know everybody else's business after awhile—no matter how lite you were, or how 'good hair', or proper-talking, you were known as having black blood, and most whites shunned you.

Tuesday, September 22

Dentist—right along behind me @ door blax man—sissy—races ahead of me into the elevator, races ahead of me again down the hall—

> Say you must be in a hurry brother.
>
> I'm in a hurry I'm late.
>
> Guess what I'm late too.

Of course seeing his black face racing in first clerk woman gets on her extra polite correct greeting—see this in a competitive sense again,

37

blax—man especially—that in this rivalry that I am @ a disadvantage.

'Trane. Saint John Coletrane, prison radio; am seated in Jasmin's car on Mission Street—she's in the fabric store obtaining costume cloth for her upcoming show audition. Here see the mad, the homeless, the drugs.

It is an overcast day today; no sun & cool.

People speaking Espanish, *Mi yamma.* Mexican music plays.

Drug weather; Autumn leaves, we need the stitches SM players pain sewing their fingers together in webs; stitch, stitch, stitch —self— punishment; we forlorn go searching sins of childhood misery.

However I am clean. Drug & alcohol free.

Sit here on Coyote stool temporarily high on trank (dentist), which will pass. Can I have a drink? No—since it never stops.

Abstinence.

Mi yamma es Rojo.

He gazed around walls Coyote; bare, stripped of artwork the former owner allowed up there, painted up to a point after that, bare cement walls discolored, and the South American ponchos which never sold. Gray & blue, cement unpainted.

Am now seated in Coyote inside—w/hot coffee & weather cool outdoors.

Wow! Sun has broken out of the clouds hot, the fades back in.

PM
PBS –listening to documentary about Alice Walker, and her lonely spearhead journey as a black woman novelist—being opposed by more traditional blax men (jealous of her fame).

Who is assembled on the road?

Those who are continuing on along w/Me.

The sun had done its worst & we had passed over into Fall.

Wednesday, September 23
Am @ Peet's coffee to use restroom & small coffee. Air conditioned!

You making a bad mistake you'll never be able to touch. In your
addiction; I'd say to them.

Am @ Coyote sit inside as 2 blax street men pests haunt the outside
being very unpleasant, also one half naked youth—dirty bare white
skin and ragged trousers; flails his skinny arms round like a
scarecrow, mumbling gibberish in a meth enhanced delusion. Drive
out customers. Sat in sunny window uncomfortable.

Perpetual problem of Miss Coyote she is situated just too far down
from affluent area, mo' near de slums, and that massive homeless
shelter—housing 4,000— run by my church, the Episcopal diocese, is
only 2 blocks away—which thrusts its unfortunate mass out of doors
from dawn until evening—locks them out—in an attempt for them to
better themselves out of doors in real life, instead of hiding in the
sanctuary. Making it quite easy for nare-do-wells to wind up here and
do their drugs and holler/scream in front of public places.

This is really like being in an outdoors mental institution.

Feel I've been looking @ ex-prison inmates who spent half a lifetime
incarnated. They are rough & tough, but not strong.

2 many bums outside—whites and black ones.

They chase away many decent men, women, trannys, just by the sight
of them.

I'll tell you one thing, I'm so tired of being poor & under-appreciated
& now old age disability. Glad I did accomplish my mega work (80

works of fiction, and now 30 Journals. ((JOURNEY, THE JOURNALS OF RED JORDAN AROBATEAU)).

A blue-tabooed white couple w/pitbull pup slides into Coyote; they are heroin fiends; slow walking, low keyed, minds elsewhere—this is the heroin weary-of-the-world look

Bible study, pastor explains covenant—way more better then a promise:

> I promise you. But I might forget all about my promise.

> We make a contract. I break my half, so this allows you to break your half as well.

> I make a covenant w/you—I will do my part—even if you fail to do your part, I will still do my part!

Wow what a deal—a covenant made to us from God! Wow!

PM
Nada.

Thursday, September 24
Ridiculous Academy of Art flag flying atop tall tall flag pole underneath the red, white, & blue.

Am @ Coyote. Sun full bright. Mid-empty. One certified dirty whiteskin bum shuffles off; w/actual purchase made in the café— from his welfare $.

So summer sun like being @ the beach; wind blows.

Rooski growls, *Da! Da!*

Seated @ Coyote now listen to this! Sky is variegated white fluffy clouds upon azure blue sky like broken up in ice floes @ the North Pole. Round sun blazing in the heavens to one corner of this tableaux.

Huge looming tekkie coach rolls past—carrying its affluent cargo amid a downtown city of poor.

40

Yum, yum, handsome older gay man walks past shirt open to the waist revealing flesh; sun—browned blond ruddy complexion of beach going. Some OGM might want to take him home—even tho he is 'over the hill' by rentboy status. Quite a handsome specimen.

Herd of 5-gangsta blax boy-men goes past making loud bangs; scary noises & anything they can to attract attention in an evil manner.

Women running to catch bus; it has gotten late, wind begins to blow. Sit here with coffee thinking how will respond tonight to tranny man e-mail about publishing my work.

Re: his offer of republishing my fine work.

Now sun has gone over building tops, its grown cold.

PM
Nada.

Friday, September 25
Found banana. Ate.

Am outside Coyote—have talked w/a few people today.

Older poet gets me laughing. W/one of his many jokes.

So many stories in this big ole city.

Oh must tell you it is good to be able to say hello to the Hawk once more, and share a wink, a joke and a nudge (a gay nudge) again, now that she has melted the riff she created, and all is @ peace between us.

PM
Correspondence w/Mitch continues he has said some good stuff about me in these emails, and where he's heard about me, is vital:

> College professors
> Gender studies professor
> Annoted bibliographys

Saturday, September 26
Walked 4 blocks today including one steep uphill slope—for exercise.
This is my day off. Body bloated from eating beef. —Intestinal
angst.

PM
Oh, this is what young Mitch emailed me:

> Your work has been overlooked in part by a complex intersection of
> classism, racism, sexism, ageism, whorephobia, homophobia and
> transphobia.

Ha! I likes dis main!

Here is my first time reading @ MCC:

> If I speak in the tongues of humans or of angels, but do not have
> love, I am only a resounding gong or a clanging cymbal. If I have
> the gift of prophecy and can fathom all mysteries and all
> knowledge, and if I have a faith that can move mountains, but do
> not have love, I am nothing. If I give all I possess to the poor and
> give over my body to hardship that I may boast, but do not have
> love, I gain nothing.
>
> Love is patient, love is kind. It does not envy, it does not boast, it is
> not proud. It does not dishonor others, it is not self-seeking, it is not
> easily angered, it keeps no record of wrongs. Love does not delight
> in evil but rejoices with the truth. It always protects, always trusts,
> always hopes, always perseveres.
>
> Love never fails. But where there are prophecies, they will cease;
> where there are tongues, they will be stilled; where there is
> knowledge, it will pass away.
> —I Corinthians 13

Sunday, September 27
Found 25¢, am putting together a dinner,

400 thousand @ Folsom Street Fair—a leather fair.

Read @ church.

Very joy inspiring music in service—felt close to God, lifted up.

PM
Emails between me and Transman Mitch ping pong back/forth, very encouraging.

Monday, September 28,
All I have to my name is $1.50.

One thing, Grace cannot be is a gay church—it is a gay inclusive but not gay—MCC is. My plan to try to go to 1 Sunday per month & read.

Blax parklet bench playing horrible rap gangsta music:

>Dat nigga pop caps in a minute.

>Eat some pussy boy.
>Eat some pussy boy.

>Black bitch.
>Black bitch.

>Dang!

Clouds of marijuana; its them—they back again.

Peaceful & safe Philippinos, transgenders & gay @ the next picnic benches—two totally different crowds.

TM PU his chair and quite obviously dragged it away from the blaxs, down to where the Flips sat in their bench conversing Taglog in low, polite voices.

TM thought he'd do what seldom did—turn round & walk back home—he had no $ for coffee—& didn't want to sit inside without no cuppa, as owners nephew there—& outside loud unpleasant thugs blowing weed fumes monopolizing the area.

Now, an old time blax gangsta goes past w/half drunk bottle of beer—large size—he really is bad news, stuck in his stupidity and insanity. On seeing him, the 5-blax youth get up and slowly & noisily depart! They don't want to be near him either!

On the walk home OM found absolutely no discarded food.

PM
Will subsist tonite on:

> 3 tangerines
> 1 can beans
> 1 can soup tortellini
> Remainder condensed milk
> Minor greens
> 2 prunes
> ¼ pk cheddar cheese

Well, hopefully will loose weight!

PPM
I showed my brokenness for the world to see.

Living alone & in poverty
--Red Jordan Arobateau
Tuesday, October 6, 2015
12:00 Midnight, Pacific Standard Time
San Francisco, CA

www.ingramcontent.com/pod-product-compliance
Lightning Source LLC
Chambersburg PA
CBHW050350290526
45785CB00006B/2710